THE DATING JOURNAL

ISBN 978-0-578-39553-1

Publisher: JL Production House
Email: thedatingjournalnyc@gmail.com

Edited by Maddie Garfinkle
Cover and page formatting by Design for Books.com

Printed in USA

THE DATING JOURNAL

The Practice of Mindful Dating

LUKE HAWKSWORTH

THE BASICS

We want to remember who our date is.

Jessica's 26, from Connecticut and works in fashion. Went to NYU. We met on Instagram — she sent me a message on IG after seeing me on Netflix's Dating Around. She's into fitness, fashion and is a foodie who likes to try new restaurants. Most of her IG is food and shots of design and architecture. About 5'7, long dark hair, pretty dark eyes and well dressed. We didn't talk much leading up to the date, went straight to the point — "when" and "where" for drinks. Had a weird feeling she might flake, so I confirmed earlier in the day that we were still on. We were. She wore a black turtleneck with a patterned skirt and leggings, elegant jewelry. We were basically matching . . . .besides the skirt.

THE PLAY BY PLAY

The details about the date.

Very solid first impression — she's beautiful and well spoken, and gave a warm hug when we met. BUT I was about 15 minutes late. It was a busy week at work and honestly my mind was all over the place. We went to Cafe Select, got a table outside with a bottle of wine. We were chatting fine, covering the basics as people do when they meet a practical stranger for dinner. When you meet someone in real life, you see the way they exist in the world — their voice, mannerisms, how they carry themselves. When you meet people online, you present yourself to each other all at once. This is always the most exciting and jarring reality for me when online dating. We talked a lot about work, which was on my mind — apparently hers too. We went on a tangent about our jobs for a while, discussing how much of life we spend in our respective offices. There were a few silent moments where I just didn't know what to say . . .I couldn't get a read on her. Did she actually think that joke I made about my childhood dog was actually funny, or was she being polite? She told me a story about her family and how they would spend summers traveling by sailboat. She misses it. She has an older brother and younger sister. She barely speaks to either. The energy seemed to be lagging a bit, and I wanted to keep it moving, so we went to my favorite spot, Soho Grand. My buddy was DJing and had a table, which always makes for a fun time. We danced a bit and got closer to each other — at least physically. It was loud so we didn't talk all that much more but I got a good feeling towards the end that we were both into each other. It got late, and it was a weeknight, so I walked her outside to call an Uber. We shared a kiss (maybe a spark, maybe the alcohol). Her car came and we wished each other a good night.

YOU ON THE DATE

Our intentions are important. Let's take a moment to recognize our own behavior—before, during and after the date.

I thought I showed up OK. Being late threw me off, I hate being late. Again, it was a long week at work so going into the date I felt a bit rushed and unprepared, slightly scattered. I think very little of my personality came out. I was either checking my email or thinking about checking my email or wondering if she was even into me. Wasn't feeling super present.

YOUR IMPRESSION

Do our values align? How did you feel ON the date

I'm definitely attracted to her. There wasn't much chemistry at first but I felt more of a connection towards the end. Could it have just been the drinks? It seems like she wants a relationship but we didn't talk about it or about past relationships and where we are with things. She seems to value family, traveling, friends and fun experiences, but we didn't go much deeper than that.

PROJECTIONS

Where do we see this going?

I could definitely bring Jess around my friends and family — my friends at Soho Grand both liked her. I didn't notice any red flags or any reason why I wouldn't want to see her again.

I'll reach out to her in a couple days to set something up because I do want to see her again. I think she wants to see me too.

Guess What . . .

. . . we never saw each other again. Why? I thought things went really well overall. What happened is what sometimes always happens: neither of us kept up communication, and we both retreated back into our separate lives. I wasn't too broken up—at the very least, I shared a fun night with someone I didn't know, one less stranger in the world. Right?

This is a guide to encourage a more mindful dating life while staying true to who you are and what your values are, in your quest to find love.

Intro

"

*Do you want to know
who you are?
Don't ask. Act!
Action will delineate
and define you.*

–THOMAS JEFFERSON

"

*Success is not final,
failure is not fatal:
it is the courage to
continue that counts.*

—WINSTON CHURCHILL

Dating is so much harder than it should be.

It is literally just two people getting dinner—why is one of them swiping on Tinder in the bathroom? Or texting their friends for an action plan of escape? Dating can feel daunting, stressful, and often overwhelming in today's increasingly digital world. The Dating Journal intends to address some of the obstacles faced internally and externally when going about finding "the right person," utilizing mindfulness to find a more intentional and fulfilling dating experience.

Some common problems with dating in a big city, and otherwise increasingly digital landscape are:

- *Access to too many options and the paradox of choice.*
- *The prevalence of hookup culture.*
- *The many forms of Situationships.*
- *Feeling too busy or distracted.*
- *Inability or confusion in knowing what you want.*
- *Fear of getting hurt.*

When facing these dating obstacles, it's not uncommon to look outwards for help—podcasts, youtube coaches, books, parents (yikes), therapists, friends in successful relationships, friends not in successful relationships, friends you didn't even ask for advice but offer it unprompted. Each source has their own, individual and strong opinions that aren't always applicable or otherwise overwhelming.

It's easy to feel defeated and overwhelmed with information and opinion, especially since some (or all) might not be relevant to YOU as an individual and your specific situation. As writer Leo Tolstoy once said, "If it is true that there are as many minds as there are heads, then there are as many kinds of love as there are hearts." In essence, everyone's needs and ideals are as specific as a fingerprint.

When going on date after date, it can turn into a cycle of forgetting the bad ones, remembering the REALLY bad ones, longing for the wrong people, or screwing up good dates for lack of confidence and constant overthinking. In my own dating trajectory, I constantly found myself wondering, Am I doing this because I'm afraid of being rejected? How can I ensure I'm not wasting my time? The Dating Journal will assist in helping you find what exactly you need (and don't), when dating towards a more fulfilling relationship and romantic life.

The stakes are high and the search for a life partner is a huge decision. So, how do we start?

First, loving yourself first is no joke. Looking inward can allow for a more solidified sense of what you need from a partner, as well as what you bring to the table in a relationship. Many of us often feel a need to be validated by those around us, to base our performance and happiness on the reactions and affirmations of others. But if your performance is contingent on external validation, you'll never feel good enough, likely keep steering towards people who are wrong for you, or hinder your own personal growth. The cognitive bias creates the need for constant validation, which withholds our ability to be vulnerable and open with those around us.

YOU are the one who holds the answers and knows yourself better than anyone else, probably more than you even realize. The Dating Journal is a practice to increase mindfulness, learn to be intentional and to create accountability in your new dating life. It will encourage you to be bold and confident, feel that you ARE enough, that you CAN make the right decisions, and that you're EXACTLY where you need to be.

And listen, **journaling?**

. . . it just *works*.

I know it can feel weird, uncomfortable, maybe even a little bit awkward. However, if you're not new to journaling, I'm sure you already know and have seen the ways in which the practice yields illuminating results. The trick? Stop overthinking. Let your thoughts flow. Use a pen, don't worry about erasing. Let go of the inevitable desire to edit, backspace, or find the right words. Journaling isn't supposed to be perfect, it's supposed to be honest. Hence why it's the first place to start when entering the battlefield of modern love.

By actively journaling your dates, you'll be more intentional with your dating trajectory, notice patterns and behavior, and gain confidence and honesty in recognizing what you really want. This journal will guide you through a personal, self-reflection that will help you discover more about yourself, develop a vision for your future, and show you how to use journaling as an effective tool towards newfound awareness in your dating life.

Past

"

Identity is a prison you can never escape, but the way to redeem your past is not to run from it, but to try to understand it, and use it as a foundation to grow.

—Jay Z

"

Learn to know yourself . . . to search realistically and regularly the processes of your own mind and feelings.

—Nelson Mandela

THE BASICS

We want to remember who our date is.

Katie is 28. Born in San Diego but grew up in a number of other countries because of her father's job. Ended up in DC and went to George Washington. She's a corporate attorney. We met on Bumble. She's tall, blond and gives off some serious Elle Woods energy (in the best way). She's also super athletic and seems like a lot of fun. Rowed crew in college and has two marathons under her (Gucci) belt.

This is the first date I've been on since my ex and I broke up. After meeting on the app, we exchanged numbers and texted for a couple weeks before finding time to meet up. I was hesitant to jump back into dating, but I knew I needed to stop avoiding it, and I was excited to meet her.

THE PLAY BY PLAY

The details about the date.

She was immediately very happy, positive and bubbly. And HOT. She looked exactly like her pictures. I invited her to a gallery opening in the neighborhood. There was an open bar, live music and fantastic people watching. She spoke intelligently about art and history, which I found charming and super attractive. I was nervous but excited. We talked a lot about traveling, work and family. I found myself avoiding the topic of my last relationship and other issues with family and work. When it came to questions about my family, I quickly breezed over them. When it came to work I acted like everything was perfect and I was doing really well, when — in truth — it's been a really tough quarter. She opened up to me about these things (her ex who she had to block, how close she is with her family) but I just couldn't reciprocate, and I found myself drifting off into thoughts of my ex.

After a couple of drinks, I started thinking TOO much about my last relationship, and got somewhat sad and distant. I noticed a painting by an artist my ex and I both liked. Katie could tell something was off. Earlier in the night she had mentioned a dessert place she liked in the neighborhood, but when the gallery opening was over, she said she needed to go home to prepare for work tomorrow. I found myself unable to say anything as she took her phone out and called an Uber. No dessert for us.

YOU ON THE DATE

Our intentions are important. Let's take a moment to recognize our own behavior—before, during and after the date.

I thought I felt good going into this date, I even bought a new outfit for this date and wanted to make a good impression. But in truth, I had been avoiding making plans. Not quite sure if I'm ready to actually date after this breakup. I felt present and engaged but I was hesitant to open up or talk about anything personal. I'm not sure if I should have actually gone on this date. I didn't feel great during it, knowing I wasn't giving her all that she was giving me, and now I feel terrible for wasting her time.

YOUR IMPRESSION

Do our values align? How did you feel ON the date

I went into the date with high hopes, but towards the end, I realized I wasn't ready and I was letting Katie down by not opening up and preventing her from really getting to know me. The attraction was there, and I think there could have been chemistry if I wasn't so distant. She was 100% looking for a relationship. She's been single for almost a year and seems like she's done a lot of work to get to a good place and ready to meet someone. She wore her values on her sleeve — hardworking, fun, excited about life and going on adventures. She loves her family and I can tell she would be an amazing partner. The whole time all I could think about is how I need to get to the same place she's at to really date again.

PROJECTIONS

Where do we see this going?

It sucks because Katie is totally someone who would get along with my friends and family. Not sure why my breakup is affecting me like this, but I'm definitely not ready to date again. I don't think she'd see me again, and that's probably for the best right now.

Can you relate . . .

Let's say you just got out of a relationship with someone you were crazy about. But now it's over. Maybe it was timing. Maybe it was just a bad situation that was stressful or emotionally damaging. Nonetheless, it's done. You're crushed, but trying to get back out there. After swiping for weeks and canceling dates, you decide to finally meet up with someone from Hinge. They look fun and approachable. Oh, and they're super hot. You get drinks at a bar in your neighborhood, and you wear that new outfit that makes you feel confident. You're nervous, but excited. The date is exactly what you expected: they look like their pictures, and they really are fun. The problem? Well, you're mostly talking about what you majored in, whether or not you like your job (you don't, but you say you do anyway—it's easier). After a few drinks, you start to get sad. Why? You miss your ex, obviously. Wait, but do you actually miss them? Or do you miss the comfort of sitting across from someone who knows you, like really knows you? This date could very well be someone you could fall in love with. What's getting in the way? Why'd you lie about liking your job when you hate it? Why'd you forget to talk about your past relationship and why you're dating again in the first place? Harnessing your past, and being honest about it, can allow for a meaningful bond to be built from the very beginning. But where do you even start?

Life is short, time flies.

In going through the motions of everyday life, it's difficult to stop and reflect on the experiences that led us to our present selves. John C. Maxwell once said "reflective thinking turns experience into insight." By taking time to actively meditate on where we came from, and the cumulative experiences that contribute to our identity, it can be easier to gain clarity on where we are, and where we're going. Particularly in regard to dating, to find your "puzzle piece," you must first know your own shape.

In the first section, we'll explore the past through questions that encourage you to reflect and share your story. To some, this might feel like a large mountain to climb. To others, a bunny slope. No one's story is the same, and everyone's comfort level regarding their past varies. The most important aspect of this exercise is to reflect in a way that brings about clarity and comfort with your personal history. Also, clarity regarding the past isn't just crucial for ourselves, but also plays an integral role in dating and getting to know someone. By understanding and getting comfortable with your own story, it's easier to share it with others.

Knowing yourself first allows you to have a clear under-standing of what you are looking for, as well as what you're bringing into a relationship. You don't need to have every-thing figured out, and sometimes examining the past raises more questions than answers, but the path to clarity begins with honesty. By coming from a place of openness and sincerity, you'll begin to have a larger understanding of who you are, and what you want.

Take a deep breath. Let's start from the beginning. Visualize yourself as a child, from your first memory, and walk through your life.

Where were you born?

What is your first memory?

What did you look forward to as a child?

How did your parents, family, and/or friends describe you?

What did you dream of when you were younger?

What were you most afraid of?

What are some obstacles you've faced?

What was the most significant event in your life thus far?

What are you most proud of?

When did you experience the most growth?

What are you grateful for in your past?

What did you learn from your parents about relationships?

What was your first crush like?

How about your first heartbreak?

How would you describe your dating life thus far?

Why did your last relationship end?

What have you learned about others through your dating history?

What have you learned about yourself?

How'd it go?

Whether it came easily or was something that required a lot of strength, take a moment to internalize these questions and your answers. Observe how you've changed over time and what caused those changes. Everything you've been through and experienced up until this point is crucial in how you will move forward, and begin to share aspects of your history with those you feel close to. Also, in reviewing your history, think about aspects of someone else's past that you would want to know in order to understand them as a person. Sometimes sharing our past can feel like an iceberg. At the top, we can talk about the basics on a first date—where we came from, what we majored in in college, our first job, etc. Underneath the iceberg might be the bigger, deeper aspects of ourselves that will require trust and partnership to share. It's okay and totally normal to stay at the top of the iceberg when getting to know someone, but remember that as you begin to trust someone, a little vulnerability goes a long way. Assess when you're ready to start sharing those other layers, and go at your own pace, because vulnerability is what builds trust and lasting partnership.

Present

"

Before I can live with other folks I've got to live with myself. The one thing that doesn't abide by majority rule is a person's conscience.

—HARPER LEE

"

Know, first, who you are, and then adorn yourself accordingly.

—EPICTETUS

THE IN BETWEEN

Time in between dates.

Hannah and I have been seeing each other for about a month now. A date per week, with some phone calls and consistent texting in between. The chemistry has been great and we make each other laugh so much, it's amazing. The phone calls are really nice. We've been facetiming this week too. There's something about her attention and sense of humor that's super comforting. I feel like we've been progressing well and getting more comfortable around each other.

THE PLAY BY PLAY

The details about the date.

I closed a big deal at work this week, Hannah was one of the first people I told. She said we should celebrate, and actually asked to take me out. It's been a long week and I was tired, but I thought it was a nice gesture. Up until this point, I've been the one making the plans and taking her out, so this was a sweet offer and change of pace. I suggested a little Italian place, Pepe Rosso, because I didn't want to go anywhere too expensive or have her feel like I was taking advantage of her gesture. She insisted on somewhere else, and replied with a screenshot of a Resy for Balthazar. Solid. I was very excited. The res was for 8pm. I arrived hungry and excited to see her, but I sat at the table alone for almost an hour, with a single text at 8:10pm saying she's running behind. She didn't get there until close to 9pm, and almost completely disregarded that she was an hour late. Anyway, I was happy to see her and besides, it was very sweet of her to offer to celebrate with me. Except all she was talking about was a new work account that was driving her insane, and didn't make any initiative to talk about the success I just had at work — which, I thought, was the whole reason for the dinner. Oh, and she started pounding glasses of wine. But whatever, I didn't want to make it a big deal, didn't have the energy. The waiter brought over more wine and, when pouring, a drop landed on Hannah's sleeve. She freaked out and scolded the waiter, calling him stupid. I tried to calm her down and helped with a napkin, but she continued to berate the waiter as he profusely apologized. She got up and stormed to the bathroom, leaving me with half a bottle of wine and half the restaurant staring. I was very thrown off. It was an accident and she treated the waiter so disrespectfully. She got back from the bathroom and I asked if she was alright, if something else was wrong, if what's happening at work has her in a bad mood. She got defensive and turned things on me, saying it wasn't a big deal until I made it a big deal. It was a very strange side of her that I don't think I've seen before, nor did I like it.

YOU ON THE DATE

Our intentions are important. Let's take a moment to recognize our own behavior—before, during and after the date.

I've been putting consistent effort into showing up to our dates with my A game, looking and feeling good. I feel like we've been spending an ample amount of time together. Not too much, not too little and keeping communication up during the times we don't see each other in person. During the date I was definitely turned off by the way she was acting. I saw an inconsiderate and rude side of her.

WHAT'S NEW

Checking in with yourself on your thoughts and intentions.

I've had the intention of progressing my relationship with Hannah and up until this point, I thought things were going great. I don't know where this side of her came from. Did I miss things during our other dates? She has a ton of great qualities and we've had a lot of fun over the past month, but something is telling me that there's something else going on. Yelling and calling the waiter stupid was a huge red flag, and she demonstrated a serious lack of compassion. The more I think about it, I realize she has been somewhat dismissive of others when we're out. Maybe I didn't notice this because I was too focused on how she was with me and the way she made me feel.

PROJECTIONS

Where do we see this going?

I'm feeling less interested in Hannah, but also confused. I definitely don't want to write her off because of one bad event, but it has me questioning more about her character. I really value kindness and compassion, and seeing Hannah's arrogance makes me wonder if she's not right for me in the long run. I'm going to see her again, but I intend on addressing the whole date, because if things do move forward, I need to understand this side of her.

Key Takeaway . . .

Listen, this side of Hannah has always been there, it's true. But it revealed itself in small doses, and I brushed it off because there were other things that overshadowed it: the sense of humor, the chemistry, the drive and ambition. But look, when it comes to lasting relationships, when there's a friction of values or character, it's not long before the dynamic reaches its inevitable end. It's also important to understand that sometimes people are in different places - level of maturity, career, or perhaps going through things in life that are affecting their behavior. It's not our job to fix the people we're dating, it is our job to recognize if we're in the same place and currently hold the same values.

"Who I Am" is a question of identity. Your identity is a cumulation of experiences, thoughts, feelings, memories, relationships, values, and beliefs that define you. Having a firm sense of identity grounds us and gives us confidence, allowing for more solidified decisions, opinions and values to live by. For many, it takes years or even an entire lifetime to discover their true identity, much of which is always changing. People are works in progress, not a final product, but having strength in values leads to strength in growth and capacity for deeper human connection.

This next portion will give you a baseline of what's important to you so that you can more easily find someone who compliments those values. By having clarity on your preferences, and a solid sense of self, you'll be able to communicate more effectively with others on what you want and need.

What are you inspired by?

What makes you laugh?

What makes you cry?

What would you say is your biggest strength?

Weakness?

How would you describe your personality?

What do you look forward to after a long day?

How do you spend your free time?

What would you do with a billion dollars?

Who do you look to during a difficult time?

What keeps you up at night?

What is something you like about yourself?

What's something you want to work on?

What are you grateful for?

What do you admire in others?

What do you deplore in others?

How is your current dating life?

What kind of people do you tend to gravitate towards?

What makes you feel close to someone?

VALUES

Life is all about decisions. Daily decisions like when/if to get out of bed, what to wear, what route to take to work, and also big picture decisions: like where to go to college, where you want your career to go, and of course who to spend your time with, date and get married to. Decision making can be stressful, especially since there are often several factors to consider. When putting your values at the forefront of any decision, the choice becomes more approachable.

In his personal values guide, author Mark Manson writes that "Values are the fundamental component of our psychological make-up and our identity. We are defined by what we choose to find important in our lives. We are defined by our prioritizations." In essence, sometimes the clearest window into our core values are our decisions. What's important to us often rules our actions and choices, so it's crucial to ensure our priorities are aligned not only with who we are now, but who we hope to become.

In dating, it's easy to push our values aside for what, in the moment, feels like a fair trade off. If you're someone who values consistency, but your partner lacks dependability, you might overlook this for something that momentarily blinds you. Let's say they have a great sense of humor, but lack honesty. Perhaps you admire their ambition, but they aren't thoughtful or compassionate. While the trade-offs seem manageable in the moment, it's an alignment of values that allows for relationships to be sustainable over time.

"Value" is a broad term, and core values can come in several forms. There are probably baseline characteristics you value in yourself and others, but by clearly defining them, it can be easier to live by them. In this next portion, review the list of values, and highlight the ones you find to be particularly crucial to being the person you are, and hope to become. Lastly, remember that this is not a complete list, but a place to start.

Values List

Authenticity	Fame	Pleasure
Achievement	Friendships	Poise
Adventure	Fun	Popularity
Authority	Growth	Recognition
Autonomy	Happiness	Religion
Balance	Honesty	Reputation
Beauty	Humor	Respect
Boldness	Influence	Responsibility
Compassion	Inner Harmony	Security
Challenge	Justice	Self-Respect
Citizenship	Kindness	Service
Community	Knowledge	Spirituality
Competency	Leadership	Stability
Contribution	Learning	Success
Creativity	Love	Status
Curiosity	Loyalty	Trustworthiness
Determination	Meaningful Work	Wealth
Experience	Openness	Wisdom
Fairness	Optimism	Other ____
Faith	Peace	

After you've gone through, reviewed, and isolated important values, take a moment to list five that are specifically prominent in your life, and why.

Value 1:

Value 2:

Value 3:

Value 4:

Value 5:

By defining core values, it'll not only help you be a stronger version of yourself, but also gain confidence in who you pursue and don't pursue romantically. Remember that if the goal is a fulfilling partnership, an alignment of character is pivotal in a lasting relationship. While in everyday life we might not be called on to be, let's say, extremely brave, or act as a leader, but it's through life's hardships that you'll want someone who can measure up to what you need from a partner, as well as someone who brings out the best of your values.

Future

"

*I dream my painting and then
I paint my dream*

—Van Gogh

THE BASICS

We want to remember who our date is.

Rachel is 25, from Long Island and went to Michigan for undergrad. She works in PR. We met on Bumble. She was pretty aggressive about setting something up. After only a few messages she said she had a reservation for dinner at Hillstone and we should meet then. I usually don't do dinner on first dates, but I went with it. She has dark hair and is super cute, but couldn't tell much else from her pictures. A lot of photos in sunglasses.

THE PLAY BY PLAY

The details about the date.

Right away I knew it was going to be a disaster. When I got to Hillstone, I had a hard time finding Rachel. When I finally did, I realized maybe her pictures hadn't been updated in a while. She was at the bar with a friend, finishing margaritas. There's nothing wrong with a pre-date cocktail, but she told me 7pm, and the reservation wasn't until 7:30. She introduced me to the friend, and said she'd be leaving before dinner. I ordered a drink and listened to Rachel and the friend gossip about work drama for 30 minutes, with little opportunity for me to join in the conversation. When the bill came, Rachel and her friend began to gather their things as the hostess told us our table was ready. I was left with the check and ended up paying for all of the drinks, which included two rounds prior to me getting there. When Rachel grabbed her bag, it was then that I noticed it wasn't just a purse, but a dog carrier with a small chihuahua in it. So the two of us — or should I say three — took a seat for dinner as Rachel kept the chihuahua next to her, feeding him small pieces of her food throughout the night. Anyway, I hardly got a full sentence in. She kept talking about her workout routine and office drama.

We did not have the same vibe or energy. She kept mentioning how her family owns a business in Long Island and she'll be moving back to her hometown to take over the business in a couple years. She also said that she loves her family, but does not want kids. All she wants is more dogs. Nothing wrong with that, but definitely not what I want.

Once we finished dinner and the server brought the bill, she stood up and said she'll meet me outside. When I got outside she said she lives a block away and asked if I wanted to come over for a Bachelor watch party at her apartment with friends. I declined.

YOU ON THE DATE

Our intentions are important. Let's take a moment to recognize our own behavior—before, during and after the date.

I was thrown off from the beginning. I guess I didn't think much of it or wasn't very intentional about a particular outcome. After the date I felt like I had wasted so much time.

YOUR IMPRESSION

Do our values align? How did you feel ON the date

What we want and who/how we are couldn't have been more different. It's hard to say what Rachels intentions were. It kinda felt like she just wanted someone to take her to dinner. This date was a good reminder to be more intentional about who I choose to go out with.

PROJECTIONS

Where do we see this going?

We won't be seeing each other again.

The Takeaway . . .

Sometimes what two people want in life doesn't align. That's ok. The important thing is that you aren't accepting other people's futures for your own—or going along for the ride in a direction you don't actually want to go because you haven't been intentional about what you want.

It's a long day at work, and you're taking a quick lunch break with a coworker. In the elevator down, the co-worker asks, "Do you want pizza or Chinese?" Distracted, or not wanting to be difficult, you say you're fine with either. "Great," says the co-worker, "let's do pizza." Wait, now you realize pizza actually sounds awful, and Chinese is really what you want. In life, we often don't know how we feel about a decision until the decision has already been made.

This anecdote highlights the consequences

of decision by indecision. In dating, when you don't have clarity on how you want your future to look, and the attributes you want your partner to have, it's easy to fall into a relationship that feels like making trade-offs based on what's already there, not what you originally hoped for yourself. With dating, once you make a decision on your future, it'll be easier to visualize yourself living out that reality or make adjustments accordingly.

If you want to date with intention, it's imperative to be intentional about your future. This starts with developing a clear and compelling vision of how you want your future to look. In the last section, you recorded your values and what matters to you most. Now, we'll align those values with a vision for the different parts of your life.

Philosopher and psychologist William James said "believe, and your belief will create the fact." By solidifying your dreams and visions, you are more consistently pulled towards them, and more likely to achieve them.

Thinking about the future not only allows for setting and achieving goals, but it's also a way of "filtering" what you do and don't want when looking for a long term partner. By knowing how you want the future to look, you can more readily find someone who aligns with and encourages your growth throughout life.

Where do you see yourself living in five years?

Do you see yourself staying in the same job or field you are in right now?

- *If not, what do you see yourself doing?*

What's something you want to accomplish throughout your life?

What do you want to improve on?

What do you want your social life to look like in ten years?

How do you envision your home when you're old?

What do you want your family life to look like? Kids? No kids? A dog?

How do you envision your future spouse or partner?

- *What's attractive about them?*

- *Why are they a good match for you?*

- *What values do they hold?*

- *What will you two do together on a rainy day?*

- *How do they complement your character and personality?*

- *What do they do when you're having a bad day?*

- *How do they support your goals and career?*

- *What are they like around your friends and family?*

- *More specifics about your ideal partner:*

What do you want most in your future relationship?

What does your life look like with your future spouse or partner?

After developing a vision, it's critical to find a way to hold yourself accountable. You are the only person in charge of your future, and while support from friends, family, and partners can help, you are ultimately the only person in charge of building the life you want. Take small steps every day that bring you an inch closer to the future you are capable of. Think of the person you want to be in five years, and start being and acting like that person today. As you went through your past section, I'm sure it was jarring to see the way time moves, and life takes shape in what feels like a blink. Future isn't much different, and it'll arrive faster than you might think.

Review the answers to your questions, and take note of small changes you have control over that might bring you a little closer to your ideal life taking shape. Accountability can be difficult, and there are several ways you can keep yourself in check. Visuals help. By seeing your answers to the questions, you've already seen the life you want stare back at you. Habitual check lists and reminders are also a good idea, especially if you're thinking about changes regarding your career or finances. Most importantly, understand and remind yourself that you deserve the life you want, acknowledge you deserve it, and continue to work for it.

Take it a step further in regard to a future relationship: summarize exactly what you want in a partner on the next page. Then rip out the page, fold it, and keep it in your purse or wallet. Bring it with you everywhere. This will serve as a constant reminder of what you want, need, and deserve.

Good Work

Mindset

"

As water reflects the face, so one's life reflects the heart.

—PROVERB

"

By three methods we may learn wisdom: First, by reflection, which is noblest; Second, by imitation, which is easiest; and third by experience which is bitterest.

—CONFUCIUS

"

Follow effective action with quiet reflection. From the quiet reflection will come even more effective action.

—PETER DRUCKER

First Date

THE BASICS

We want to remember who our date is.

Isabella is 24, she's Italian and has been in NYC for about 10 years with her family who lives in Brooklyn. She lives in Chelsea, works for a real estate developer, and has a French Bulldog named Leo — among other cute pet names she calls him. She loves checking things off her bucket list, traveling and taking vacations with big groups and family. Lisa, my co-worker, had been saying we should go out for weeks now but I'd been hesitant after my recent bout of seven terrible dates in a row. Nonetheless, I trust my coworker, so I agreed and tried to be optimistic.

THE PLAY BY PLAY

The details about the date.

When setting up the date, we challenged each other to pick a spot with the best espresso martini. Being a Friday night and after a long work week, it made sense. I picked Lola Taverna. Great atmosphere, food is amazing and the espresso martinis have the best foam in the city. It's all about the foam. Anyway, we met around 9pm and sat at the bar. My co-worker described Isabella as funny, hardworking, and close with her family. She was all of those things. Almost too good to be true. After coming out of a 3 month relationship with a toxic ending and having so many bad dates in a row, I felt somewhat skeptical though. I kept asking myself: what's wrong with her? There's no way this girl is perfect. Also, it reminded me of when I first met my last ex — everything seemed perfect, and it wasn't until later that the perfection started to wear off, and she revealed herself to be a completely different person. These thoughts definitely got in the way of me learning more about Isabella. It felt like I was meeting someone I could actually see myself getting along with, but I found myself putting up a wall.

We finished drinks and decided to hop over to Butterfly, where some of my friends were. We had a drink there, but then she mentioned wanting to meet up with some of her friends nearby, and said she wanted to go on her own. I don't know if it was a self-fulfilling prophecy or what, but part of me had a feeling it'd end this way.

YOU ON THE DATE

Our intentions are important. Let's take a moment to recognize our own behavior—before, during and after the date.

I feel like I showed up well to the date. I was feeling good. However, looking back, I realize I went into the night with a pessimistic mindset after my last relationship and the recent bad dates. Initially, I thought her decision to go out with her friends was predictable and even expected, but looking back, I realize the stakes I had in where the direction of the night went. While Isabella made the call to part ways, it may have had something to do with how absent I seemed and my hesitance to be vulnerable. Even though I thought I looked and felt good, I wasn't being totally honest with myself about how much I was dreading the night, and I'm sure that negativity was shown throughout the evening.

YOUR IMPRESSION

Do our values align? How did you feel ON the date

I thought we could have had chemistry, but I didn't let it develop. I could tell she had good values and a solid character. She was looking for something serious, but my head just wasn't in it.

PROJECTIONS

Where do we see this going?

Unfortunately, I don't see this going anywhere. I feel like I could try for a second date and show up with a better mindset but I might just need more time.

Can you relate . . .

Things with your ex ended—probably for the best. Now you're getting back out there (again). The break up with your ex was hard, but it taught you a lot about what you're looking for in terms of character. You realized how much compassion and active listening are important to you. You agree to finally let your co-worker set you up with their friend. They've been raving for weeks about how much she thinks you two will get along. You weren't really ready to get back out there, I mean, things with the ex kind of sent you for a tailspin and you're still a little emotionally whiplashed. You went on a few dates after the ex, but they were all awful. You're starting to feel like dating is hopeless, and there's no quality prospects left in the whole world. No getting around it: it sucks right now. But the co-worker keeps insisting, and says their friend is funny, hardworking, and close with their family. It all sounds perfect, why not just try? You agree, and a plan is set for Friday. When Friday comes, you are just so not in the mood. You make yourself a cocktail before heading over to the restaurant, where you also have two more cocktails. The friend is amazing. Super kind and intelligent. They're asking you the questions. They want to hear about your family. You barely notice this, because the whole time you're looking for flaws, or red flags that might show up later. Why should you trust this person? Why should you believe they won't end up exactly like your last partner or everyone else who let you down? **The truth is, you have no idea. But your tainted mindset going into the date has already damaged or hindered any possibility for you to see goodness or potential in this person. In essence: it was doomed from the start, because you were afraid to believe it could be anything else.**

One tell-tale sign of being ready—or not ready—to date, is your headspace surrounding prospective dates and dating in general. If you're still hooked on your ex, or hesitant because of past experiences, there's a lot of pressure that goes into dates, and the outcome will likely be unfavorable. Alternatively, if you take time to heal, reflect, and adopt an open mind and a positive mindset, dating can be a positive experience. By being intentional and vulnerable when dating, chances are that the other person will instinctively feel more comfortable letting their guard down as well.

Validation plays a huge role in our interactions, relationships, and self esteem. It can often get in the way of a healthy mindset, as the strive for validation might warp your mindset towards the wrong things. Sometimes when we're in a low place with ourselves, it can be easy to be driven by external validation, but this hinders growth and can leave us stunted in regard to what we actually need from another person. Validation will always play a role in our lives, and a healthy amount of affirmation isn't always a bad thing, but it's important to take a moment and consider where the need to feel accepted is coming from.

If dating is particularly daunting at the moment, an approachable mindset is the mentality of genuine curiosity. If you go into a date with the curiosity of getting to know another person, you'll leave the experience with— at the very least—one less stranger in the world. Dating can be stressful, dreadful, and really dang hard, but when you consider how cool it is, really, to sit across from someone who exists in a completely different world, it can be an awesome experience to get to know a stranger. When the baseline is curiosity, it's not all that bad, and the added bonus is that you two might hit it off.

If you feel you're ready to date, be extremely intentional and find your person, you can take this curiosity one step further. Think about what exactly it is about this person that draws you to them before the date. Consider what you're looking forward to hearing more about, and what you're excited to share.

Generally, a fearful or pessimistic mindset can be the single most powerful thing that deters one's dating trajectory. If it still seems difficult to be positive going into a date, it's probably a sign that more reflecting or healing needs to happen before getting back out there—and that's okay. It can take a really long time to feel "ready," but when you finally do, having a healthy outlook will yield more positive experiences and attract the right people for you.

Another important thing to consider is your date's mindset. For the record, it's totally not weird to be like, How's it going on Hinge? Or: how's your dating experience been? It can often relieve the pressure by addressing the "elephant in the room," because at the end of the day, you're both there for a reason. This can also reveal how comfortable someone is in talking about these things, and see where you two align, or don't. Alternatively, after the initial stages of getting to know each other, it might be time to feel out or discuss their current mindset regarding where things are going. A confident approach is the best approach. This is absolutely crucial, especially when you're ready to be serious about dating. If you find someone you really get along with, and see it going somewhere, but they are in a more casual phase or stuck in thinking only about the present, it might be time to pivot towards something that aligns more with your current mindset.

Lastly, it's okay if you don't entirely feel ready to accept the mindset needed to be in a fulfilling relationship. One way to take the temperature of your current mindset regarding dating is how willing you are to take on something "good." It can be really easy, especially after being hurt or disappointed, to be prepared for the worst, and accept something "bad." When people mistreat us and let us down, it's often "safer," because in the end, we probably know it doesn't require that much from us emotionally, because they don't give us much emotionally. Sometimes the scariest thing is meeting someone who is good, kind, and compatible with you, in a time when you don't feel worthy or ready. Oftentimes, it can be a difficult truth to realize you're not ready for something right, and take this as a signal to return to thoughtful reflection until you know, for certain, you're in the mindset to accept treatment you deserve, not just treatment you know how to handle.

MAIN TAKEAWAYS:

Dating is an exciting opportunity.

Be Excited.

Be Positive.

Be Curious.

Be Bold.

Be Confident.

The more you give, the more you get.

Journal

> **"**
>
> *Love is an action first,*
> *it's a feeling second.*
>
> —DR. TIMOTHY KELLER

First Date

THE BASICS

We want to remember who our date is.

Anna is 27, she grew up in North Carolina about two hours away from where I grew up. Her family still lives there. She has a younger brother named Charlie. She lives in Greenwich Village, is an accountant and runs her own tax strategy business. Tall, dirty blonde hair with blue eyes. Intelligent, elegant, sophisticated yet approachable. She enjoys the opera, the arts and film like I do. Likes the outdoors. Loves live music and plays the piano.

We met at a charity event last Saturday. It was near the end of the night and we were standing next to each other at the bar. I overheard her talking to her friend and saying the word "Y'all." I turned to her and said "Someone's from the south." "Takes a southerner to know one," she replied. We chatted briefly, then I asked for her number and said I'd like to take her out. She said she'd like that. I called her the next day and asked when she was free.

THE PLAY BY PLAY

The details about the date.

I was reminded of a line from one of my favorite movies, Hitch with Will Smith, when he says "No woman wakes up saying 'god I hope I don't get swept off my feet today.'" I got such a good feeling when I met Anna. It's been months of dating without meeting someone and feeling a true connection, so I wanted to put my best foot forward. A past client of mine was hosting a Sofar Sounds concert at his townhouse in West Village for an up and coming singer and pianist. Offering to be a gentleman, I told Anna I would pick her up in an Uber at 8pm. Noone does that anymore. We went to one of my favorite cocktail bars called Little Branch first, so we could have some one on one time before the event. She was well spoken and confident and I could tell she really listened when I was talking. Things were so smooth. We told stories, laughed together and shared some vulnerable moments when talking about past relationships and where we currently are in life. She talked about her friends a lot, who she seems to be very close with. Her parents are no longer together and she opened up about that. Has a couple travel plans coming up and seems to be very adventurous — went skydiving and scuba diving on her last trip.

We headed to the event and had a blast. She has no trouble meeting new people and keeping conversation. She laughs A LOT. How is this girl so happy!? Also she keeps such good eye contact when in conversation and really notices things. After the performance, we went out on the terrace together. We talked about how nice the townhouse was and she mentioned how she can't wait to have a place like this. She said she sees herself staying in NYC and having a family here. Ambitious. And exactly what I want. Before leaving, my client stopped Anna and I and invited us to a dinner he's having next week. She answered confidently for both of us, "we'll be there."

I called an Uber to her place, walked her to her door and we shared a kiss. It was a great night. I just sent her flowers.

YOU ON THE DATE

Our intentions are important. Let's take a moment to recognize our own behavior—before, during and after the date.

I knew I wanted to make the most out of our date, so I really prepared. I got a haircut the day prior, wore one of my best outfits, and felt great. I tried to be very positive and genuine and very open with her. I don't think there's anything I could have done differently. Reflecting on this date, I feel very good about it and can't wait to see Anna again.

YOUR IMPRESSION

Do our values align? How did you feel ON the date

The chemistry was pretty obvious and I could tell we both wanted to be there. She said she's been single for over 6 months and was very up front about her intentions, wanting a relationship and something serious. Maybe it had something to do with growing up in the same general area but we shared the same values, and had similar belief systems. We both aren't crazy about politics but are passionate about certain issues and have the desire to be more and more involved in philanthropy.

PROJECTIONS

Where do we see this going?

I see this going the distance. I am very interested in getting to know Anna more. I think my friends and family would love her. No red flags that I can tell. I 100% want to see her again and I think she wants to see me again too.

The Takeaway . . .

We've Done The Work. We have a hold on our Past, Confidence about Who We Are and our Values, we have a Vision for our Future, and a Positive Mindset.

The foundation you've just created will

be fundamental moving forward. By acknowledging your past, present, future, and mindset, journaling will be that much easier and illuminating. Quite frankly, journaling only works when you fully commit: be vulnerable, and let your mind flow. Remember: it just *works*. But only if you want it to. By journaling your dates and the thoughts surrounding them, you'll be more intentional and fulfilled in finding a partner. Whether you already journal regularly, or this will be your first, the intention is the same for veterans and novices alike: structure. By having a defined and consistent structure to record and review your dates, you'll more quickly and insightfully acknowledge patterns, and adopt a more intentional approach to dating and finding your person.

The following template and questions are intended to tease out more specificity than you would otherwise. By documenting crucial date details, it'll bring to light what works for you and doesn't, paving a clearer path to your ideal match. Also, it's no secret: dating, especially these days, is totally a numbers game. A lot of dates are boring, or only okay. Remember that sometimes you'll need to go on a lot of dates to find one that feels promising. Don't get discouraged. Document the ones that are fine, bad, or just plain boring. There's something to learn from each and every one, and the whole point of this process is to show you that. Lastly, journaling is only half of the work. Remember to reflect and review your dates as you continue on your dating journey.

The following template includes questions you will answer after each FIRST date. Refer back to this template before journaling. Be as detailed or creative as you'd like, and don't be afraid to add additional questions or points you want to track throughout your dating journey. When journaling, allow these questions to stimulate your subconscious as you record the details of the date and uncover your feelings about it.

Did you meet someone IRL (in real life) and have a meaningful time? Use the First Date entry to reflect on this experience too.

Having trouble finding things to talk about on your date? Use these questions as a way to spark the conversation. Review prior so you are ready with everything you want to learn and prioritize.

There are 20 First Date entries. There are an additional 20 entries to journal your 2nd, 3rd, 4th etc dates. Have fun, be honest, and be prepared to meet your match!

FIRST DATE TEMPLATE

Name: _____ **First Date** ___/___/20___

THE BASICS

We want to remember who our date is and their details.

- *Age:*
- *Where are they from(hometown):*
- *Occupation:*
- *Where did you initially meet?:*
- *Overall appearance:*
- *What are their hobbies?:*
- *Communication leading up to the date*

THE PLAY BY PLAY

The details about the date.

- *What was your first impression of this person?*
- *Where did you go and what did you do?:*
- *How did the conversation flow?:*
- *Were there any meaningful or vulnerable moments?:*
- *Did you have a good time?:*

YOU ON THE DATE

Our intentions are important. Let's take a moment to recognize our own behavior – before, during and after the date.

- ▶ *Your appearance?*
- ▶ *How did you feel going into the date?*
- ▶ *What side of your personality came out during the date?*
- ▶ *Did you feel present?*
- ▶ *How did you feel after the date?*
- ▶ *Anything you could have done differently?*

YOUR IMPRESSION

Do our values align? How did you feel ON the date

- ▶ *How did you feel on the date?*
- ▶ *Did you have chemistry (physical, mental, emotional)?*
- ▶ *What do you feel are your date's intentions?/ Are you looking for the same level of commitment?*
- ▶ *What do you feel their core values are?*
- ▶ *What about the date are you grateful for?*

PROJECTIONS

Where do we see this going?

- ▶ *Could you bring this person around your friends & family?*
- ▶ *Do you feel more or less interested in the person now?*
- ▶ *Would you see this person again?*
- ▶ *Were there any potential red flags or deal breakers you noticed?*
- ▶ *Do you think your date would want to see you again?*

Name: _____ **First Date** ___/___/20___

THE BASICS

We want to remember who our date is.

THE PLAY BY PLAY

The details about the date.

YOU ON THE DATE

Our intentions are important. Let's take a moment to recognize our own behavior—before, during and after the date.

YOUR IMPRESSION

Do our values align? How did you feel ON the date

PROJECTIONS

Where do we see this going?

Name: _____ **First Date** ___/___/20____

THE BASICS

We want to remember who our date is.

THE PLAY BY PLAY

The details about the date.

YOU ON THE DATE

Our intentions are important. Let's take a moment to recognize our own behavior—before, during and after the date.

YOUR IMPRESSION

Do our values align? How did you feel ON the date

PROJECTIONS

Where do we see this going?

Name: _____ **First Date** __/__/20____

THE BASICS

We want to remember who our date is.

THE PLAY BY PLAY

The details about the date.

YOU ON THE DATE

Our intentions are important. Let's take a moment to recognize our own behavior—before, during and after the date.

YOUR IMPRESSION

Do our values align? How did you feel ON the date

PROJECTIONS

Where do we see this going?

Name: _____ **First Date** ___/ ___/20____

THE BASICS

We want to remember who our date is.

THE PLAY BY PLAY

The details about the date.

YOU ON THE DATE

Our intentions are important. Let's take a moment to recognize our own behavior—before, during and after the date.

YOUR IMPRESSION

Do our values align? How did you feel ON the date

PROJECTIONS

Where do we see this going?

Name: _____   **First Date**   __/__/20____

THE BASICS

We want to remember who our date is.

THE PLAY BY PLAY

The details about the date.

YOU ON THE DATE

Our intentions are important. Let's take a moment to recognize our own behavior—before, during and after the date.

YOUR IMPRESSION

Do our values align? How did you feel ON the date

PROJECTIONS

Where do we see this going?

First Date

THE BASICS

We want to remember who our date is.

THE PLAY BY PLAY

The details about the date.

YOU ON THE DATE

Our intentions are important. Let's take a moment to recognize our own behavior—before, during and after the date.

YOUR IMPRESSION

Do our values align? How did you feel ON the date

PROJECTIONS

Where do we see this going?

Name: _____   **First Date**   __/__/20____

THE BASICS

We want to remember who our date is.

THE PLAY BY PLAY

The details about the date.

YOU ON THE DATE

Our intentions are important. Let's take a moment to recognize our own behavior—before, during and after the date.

YOUR IMPRESSION

Do our values align? How did you feel ON the date

PROJECTIONS

Where do we see this going?

Name: _____ **First Date** ___/___/20____

THE BASICS

We want to remember who our date is.

THE PLAY BY PLAY

The details about the date.

YOU ON THE DATE

Our intentions are important. Let's take a moment to recognize our own behavior—before, during and after the date.

YOUR IMPRESSION

Do our values align? How did you feel ON the date

PROJECTIONS

Where do we see this going?

First Date

___/ ___/20____

THE BASICS

We want to remember who our date is.

THE PLAY BY PLAY

The details about the date.

YOU ON THE DATE

Our intentions are important. Let's take a moment to recognize our own behavior—before, during and after the date.

YOUR IMPRESSION

Do our values align? How did you feel ON the date

PROJECTIONS

Where do we see this going?

Name: _____ **First Date** ___/___/20___

THE BASICS

We want to remember who our date is.

THE PLAY BY PLAY

The details about the date.

YOU ON THE DATE

Our intentions are important. Let's take a moment to recognize our own behavior—before, during and after the date.

YOUR IMPRESSION

Do our values align? How did you feel ON the date

PROJECTIONS

Where do we see this going?

Name: _____ **First Date** ___/___/20___

THE BASICS

We want to remember who our date is.

THE PLAY BY PLAY

The details about the date.

YOU ON THE DATE

Our intentions are important. Let's take a moment to recognize our own behavior—before, during and after the date.

YOUR IMPRESSION

Do our values align? How did you feel ON the date

PROJECTIONS

Where do we see this going?

Name: _____ **First Date** ___/___/20____

THE BASICS

We want to remember who our date is.

THE PLAY BY PLAY

The details about the date.

YOU ON THE DATE

Our intentions are important. Let's take a moment to recognize our own behavior—before, during and after the date.

YOUR IMPRESSION

Do our values align? How did you feel ON the date

PROJECTIONS

Where do we see this going?

Name: _____ **First Date** ___/___/20___

THE BASICS

We want to remember who our date is.

THE PLAY BY PLAY

The details about the date.

YOU ON THE DATE

Our intentions are important. Let's take a moment to recognize our own behavior—before, during and after the date.

YOUR IMPRESSION

Do our values align? How did you feel ON the date

PROJECTIONS

Where do we see this going?

Name: _____ **First Date** ___/___/20____

THE BASICS

We want to remember who our date is.

THE PLAY BY PLAY

The details about the date.

YOU ON THE DATE

Our intentions are important. Let's take a moment to recognize our own behavior—before, during and after the date.

YOUR IMPRESSION

Do our values align? How did you feel ON the date

PROJECTIONS

Where do we see this going?

Name: _____ **First Date** ___/ ___/20_____

THE BASICS

We want to remember who our date is.

THE PLAY BY PLAY

The details about the date.

YOU ON THE DATE

Our intentions are important. Let's take a moment to recognize our own behavior—before, during and after the date.

YOUR IMPRESSION

Do our values align? How did you feel ON the date

PROJECTIONS

Where do we see this going?

First Date

THE BASICS

We want to remember who our date is.

THE PLAY BY PLAY

The details about the date.

YOU ON THE DATE

Our intentions are important. Let's take a moment to recognize our own behavior—before, during and after the date.

YOUR IMPRESSION

Do our values align? How did you feel ON the date

PROJECTIONS

Where do we see this going?

Name: _____ **First Date** ___/___/20____

THE BASICS

We want to remember who our date is.

THE PLAY BY PLAY

The details about the date.

YOU ON THE DATE

Our intentions are important. Let's take a moment to recognize our own behavior—before, during and after the date.

YOUR IMPRESSION

Do our values align? How did you feel ON the date

PROJECTIONS

Where do we see this going?

First Date

THE BASICS

We want to remember who our date is.

THE PLAY BY PLAY

The details about the date.

YOU ON THE DATE

Our intentions are important. Let's take a moment to recognize our own behavior—before, during and after the date.

YOUR IMPRESSION

Do our values align? How did you feel ON the date

PROJECTIONS

Where do we see this going?

Name: _____ **First Date** ___/___/20____

THE BASICS

We want to remember who our date is.

THE PLAY BY PLAY

The details about the date.

YOU ON THE DATE

Our intentions are important. Let's take a moment to recognize our own behavior—before, during and after the date.

YOUR IMPRESSION

Do our values align? How did you feel ON the date

PROJECTIONS

Where do we see this going?

Name: _____ **First Date** ___/ ___/20____

THE BASICS

We want to remember who our date is.

THE PLAY BY PLAY

The details about the date.

YOU ON THE DATE

Our intentions are important. Let's take a moment to recognize our own behavior—before, during and after the date.

YOUR IMPRESSION

Do our values align? How did you feel ON the date

PROJECTIONS

Where do we see this going?

TEMPLATE FOR 2ND, 3RD, 4TH ETC DATES

Name: _____   **Date #** __   __/__/20___

THE IN BETWEEN

Time in between dates.

- ▶ *What happened between dates? Texting? Who asked who out?*

THE PLAY BY PLAY

The details about the date.

- ▶ *Where did you go and what did you do?:*
- ▶ *Did you have a good time?:*

YOU ON THE DATE

Our intentions are important. Let's take a moment to recognize our own behavior—before, during and after the date.

- ▶ *Your appearance?:*
- ▶ *How did you feel going into the date?*
- ▶ *During the Date?*

WHAT'S NEW

Checking in with yourself on your thoughts and intentions.

- ▶ *Why did you decide to go on a second date with this person?*
- ▶ *What was something new about this person that you learned?*
- ▶ *So far, what is something you admire about this person and something you notice that you don't like as much?*
- ▶ *Did your connection with this person grow?*
- ▶ *What moments stood out to you?*
- ▶ *How did the relationship progress?*

PROJECTIONS

Where do we see this going?

- ▶ *Do you feel more or less interested in the person now?*
- ▶ *Would you see this person again?*
- ▶ *Were there any potential red flags or deal breakers you noticed?*
- ▶ *Do you think your date would want to see you again?*

Name: _____   **Date #** __   __/__/20___

THE IN BETWEEN

Time in between dates.

THE PLAY BY PLAY

The details about the date.

YOU ON THE DATE

Our intentions are important. Let's take a moment to recognize our own behavior—before, during and after the date.

WHAT'S NEW

Checking in with yourself on your thoughts and intentions.

PROJECTIONS

Where do we see this going?

THE IN BETWEEN

Time in between dates.

THE PLAY BY PLAY

The details about the date.

YOU ON THE DATE

Our intentions are important. Let's take a moment to recognize our own behavior—before, during and after the date.

WHAT'S NEW

Checking in with yourself on your thoughts and intentions.

PROJECTIONS

Where do we see this going?

THE IN BETWEEN

Time in between dates.

THE PLAY BY PLAY

The details about the date.

YOU ON THE DATE

Our intentions are important. Let's take a moment to recognize our own behavior—before, during and after the date.

WHAT'S NEW

Checking in with yourself on your thoughts and intentions.

PROJECTIONS

Where do we see this going?

Name: _____   **Date #** __   __/__/20___

THE IN BETWEEN

Time in between dates.

THE PLAY BY PLAY

The details about the date.

YOU ON THE DATE

Our intentions are important. Let's take a moment to recognize our own behavior—before, during and after the date.

WHAT'S NEW

Checking in with yourself on your thoughts and intentions.

PROJECTIONS

Where do we see this going?

THE IN BETWEEN

Time in between dates.

THE PLAY BY PLAY

The details about the date.

YOU ON THE DATE

Our intentions are important. Let's take a moment to recognize our own behavior—before, during and after the date.

WHAT'S NEW

Checking in with yourself on your thoughts and intentions.

PROJECTIONS

Where do we see this going?

Name: _____ **Date # __** __/__/20___

THE IN BETWEEN
Time in between dates.

THE PLAY BY PLAY
The details about the date.

YOU ON THE DATE

Our intentions are important. Let's take a moment to recognize our own behavior—before, during and after the date.

WHAT'S NEW

Checking in with yourself on your thoughts and intentions.

PROJECTIONS

Where do we see this going?

THE IN BETWEEN

Time in between dates.

THE PLAY BY PLAY

The details about the date.

YOU ON THE DATE

Our intentions are important. Let's take a moment to recognize our own behavior—before, during and after the date.

WHAT'S NEW

Checking in with yourself on your thoughts and intentions.

PROJECTIONS

Where do we see this going?

THE IN BETWEEN

Time in between dates.

THE PLAY BY PLAY

The details about the date.

YOU ON THE DATE

Our intentions are important. Let's take a moment to recognize our own behavior—before, during and after the date.

WHAT'S NEW

Checking in with yourself on your thoughts and intentions.

PROJECTIONS

Where do we see this going?

THE IN BETWEEN

Time in between dates.

THE PLAY BY PLAY

The details about the date.

YOU ON THE DATE

Our intentions are important. Let's take a moment to recognize our own behavior—before, during and after the date.

WHAT'S NEW

Checking in with yourself on your thoughts and intentions.

PROJECTIONS

Where do we see this going?

Name: _____ **Date #** __   __/ __/20___

THE IN BETWEEN

Time in between dates.

THE PLAY BY PLAY

The details about the date.

YOU ON THE DATE

Our intentions are important. Let's take a moment to recognize our own behavior—before, during and after the date.

WHAT'S NEW

Checking in with yourself on your thoughts and intentions.

PROJECTIONS

Where do we see this going?

Name: _____ **Date #** __   __/__/20___

THE IN BETWEEN

Time in between dates.

THE PLAY BY PLAY

The details about the date.

YOU ON THE DATE

Our intentions are important. Let's take a moment to recognize our own behavior—before, during and after the date.

WHAT'S NEW

Checking in with yourself on your thoughts and intentions.

PROJECTIONS

Where do we see this going?

THE IN BETWEEN

Time in between dates.

THE PLAY BY PLAY

The details about the date.

YOU ON THE DATE

Our intentions are important. Let's take a moment to recognize our own behavior—before, during and after the date.

WHAT'S NEW

Checking in with yourself on your thoughts and intentions.

PROJECTIONS

Where do we see this going?

THE IN BETWEEN

Time in between dates.

THE PLAY BY PLAY

The details about the date.

YOU ON THE DATE

Our intentions are important. Let's take a moment to recognize our own behavior—before, during and after the date.

WHAT'S NEW

Checking in with yourself on your thoughts and intentions.

PROJECTIONS

Where do we see this going?

Name: _____ Date # __ ___/ __/20 ___

THE IN BETWEEN

Time in between dates.

THE PLAY BY PLAY

The details about the date.

YOU ON THE DATE

Our intentions are important. Let's take a moment to recognize our own behavior—before, during and after the date.

WHAT'S NEW

Checking in with yourself on your thoughts and intentions.

PROJECTIONS

Where do we see this going?

Name: _____   **Date # __**   __/ __/20___

THE IN BETWEEN

Time in between dates.

THE PLAY BY PLAY

The details about the date.

YOU ON THE DATE

Our intentions are important. Let's take a moment to recognize our own behavior—before, during and after the date.

WHAT'S NEW

Checking in with yourself on your thoughts and intentions.

PROJECTIONS

Where do we see this going?

Name: _____   **Date # __**   __/__/20____

THE IN BETWEEN

Time in between dates.

THE PLAY BY PLAY

The details about the date.

YOU ON THE DATE

Our intentions are important. Let's take a moment to recognize our own behavior—before, during and after the date.

WHAT'S NEW

Checking in with yourself on your thoughts and intentions.

PROJECTIONS

Where do we see this going?

Name: _____ **Date #** __   __/__/20____

THE IN BETWEEN

Time in between dates.

THE PLAY BY PLAY

The details about the date.

YOU ON THE DATE

Our intentions are important. Let's take a moment to recognize our own behavior—before, during and after the date.

WHAT'S NEW

Checking in with yourself on your thoughts and intentions.

PROJECTIONS

Where do we see this going?

THE IN BETWEEN

Time in between dates.

THE PLAY BY PLAY

The details about the date.

YOU ON THE DATE

Our intentions are important. Let's take a moment to recognize our own behavior—before, during and after the date.

WHAT'S NEW

Checking in with yourself on your thoughts and intentions.

PROJECTIONS

Where do we see this going?

THE IN BETWEEN

Time in between dates.

THE PLAY BY PLAY

The details about the date.

YOU ON THE DATE

Our intentions are important. Let's take a moment to recognize our own behavior—before, during and after the date.

WHAT'S NEW

Checking in with yourself on your thoughts and intentions.

PROJECTIONS

Where do we see this going?

THE IN BETWEEN

Time in between dates.

THE PLAY BY PLAY

The details about the date.

YOU ON THE DATE

Our intentions are important. Let's take a moment to recognize our own behavior—before, during and after the date.

WHAT'S NEW

Checking in with yourself on your thoughts and intentions.

PROJECTIONS

Where do we see this going?

Acknowledgments

When I first sat down to write my acknowledgements I had the bright idea to jokingly say "Thank you to all my ex's & my Mother." But after thinking about it, I realized . . . it wasn't a joke at all. It was the truth. And an accompanying truth was that I once again thought to use humor to cover up the vulnerable areas of my life. Some of my past relationships and family life are filled with brokenness and painful moments where I've felt the most vulnerable. Often, my first instinct has been to run from these vulnerable moments, suppress them with humor or indifference and carry on like everything has and will always be ok. But I'm tired of running. I want to own my pain and vulnerability because it's in these moments we experience growth.. and I'm choosing to grow, be bold, hopeful, confident and live a life full of passion.

A very special thank you to Maddie, my very talented editor, who transformed my chicken scratch vision into what it is today.

Thank you to my book designer Michael at Design For Books for the amazing work.

Thank you to my good friend and productivity coach Anthony, who inspired me to keep moving forward.

Thank you to my Mother and Father for their love and the gift of opportunity.

My friends who have supported me, believed in me, and gave me hell along the way: Dustin G, Alec, Mikayla, Max, Cole, Nader, Danny, Mike L, Enzo, my Dating Around sister Gurki, Keith who when I told I was writing a book replied "have you tried reading one", Andrew & Kristin, Bobby, David D, David P, Patrick Y, & Berg.

Matt H, who is missed tremendously but is the reason I live life to the fullest. Beth & Dave who have been a rock.

My brother Matthew who's strength, faith & discipline I admire greatly.

Lastly, this book is for my Wife. I don't know who you are yet or where we'll find each other but I can't wait to meet you. I can't wait to fall in love and build a beautiful family together. I can't wait to laugh with you and cry with you, for the good experiences and to support each other through the difficult ones. I promise that each and every day I'm doing the work to get one step closer to you. I pray for your safety, health, joy & peace and that we will meet one day soon.

About The Author

New York City based real estate entrepreneur, actor and author, Luke Hawksworth, gained public recognition through his Netflix debut of *Dating Around*. This experience led to Luke searching for answers to the many struggles people face today in modern dating. Noticing the abundance of dating advice that rarely has long lasting impact, Luke takes a practical approach to finding our match by encouraging singles to be intentional and to Do The Work.

Made in the USA
Las Vegas, NV
14 February 2023

67543810R00092